W9-ABH-128

98

j535
TOM

Tomecek, Steve.
Bouncing and
bending light

HAYNER PUBLIC LIBRARY DISTRICT
ALTON, ILLINOIS

OVERDUES .10 PER DAY. MAXIMUM FINE
COST OF BOOKS. LOST OR DAMAGED BOOKS
ADDITIONAL $5.00 SERVICE CHARGE.

DEMCO

BOUNCING & BENDING LIGHT

PHANTASTIC PHYSICAL PHENOMENA™

by Steve Tomecek

pictures by Arnie Ten

Scientific American
BOOKS FOR YOUNG READERS

W. H. Freeman and Company
New York

HAYNER PUBLIC LIBRARY DISTRICT
ALTON, ILLINOIS

To Christy, Stephen Jr., and especially my wife, Lynn, who shared in my dreams and helped make the reality.—S. T.

To Charles and Nathanael—A.T.

Phantastic Physical Phenomena™ is a trademark and service mark of Louisiana Public Broadcasting.

Text copyright © 1995 by Steve Tomecek.

Illustrations copyright © 1995 by Arnie Ten.

All rights reserved. No part of this book may be reproduced by any mechanical, photographic, or electronic process, or in the form of a phonographic or digital recording, nor may it be stored in a retrieval system, transmitted, or otherwise copied for public or private use, without the written permission of the publisher.

Book design by Maria Epes.

Scientific American Books for Young Readers is an imprint of W. H. Freeman and Company, 41 Madison Avenue, New York, New York 10010.

Tomecek, Steve.

    Fun with bouncing and bending light / Steve Tomecek.

        p.   cm.

    ISBN 0-7167-6541-1.—ISBN 0-7167-6591-8 (pbk.)

    1. Light—Juvenile literature. 2. Light—Experiments—Juvenile literature. 3. Reflection (Optics)—Juvenile literature. 4. Reflection (Optics)—Experiments—Juvenile literature. [1. Light—Experiments. 2. Reflection (Optics)—Experiments. 3. Experiments.]

QC360.T66 1995

535'.078—dc20

94-37820

CIP

AC

Printed in the United States of America

    10 9 8 7 6 5 4 3 2 1

Acs-0319

Table of Contents

Introduction

When you think of "Science," the first thing you may think of is a bunch of facts that explain why things happen the way they do. While facts are central to science, it's important to remember that facts can change! Five hundred years ago, it was a scientific fact that Earth was flat and that the sun, the stars, and the planets all revolved around it. The true beauty of science isn't just learning the facts, it's the *process* of figuring out why stuff happens. Scientists never have all the answers. As technology changes and we get new information, scientific "facts" change too.

The Phantastic Physical Phenomena series looks at science as more than a collection of facts. By presenting experiments, I will challenge you to come up with your own facts about how the world behaves. In addition, so you can see how science changes, I will talk about some of the great men and women in the history of science who weren't afraid to challenge the facts in search of the truth.

As you move through this book and try out the experiments, you will find some facts, but you'll have to figure out how to read them! If you're stumped, just take a look in a mirror for a clue! Remember that in science, there are no right answers, just new facts waiting to be discovered.

1
How Does Light Bounce?

Picture this if you can. You're walking down the street doing a little window shopping when suddenly you see your own face staring back at you from inside the store. Or perhaps you're out strolling after a rainstorm, hopping from puddle to puddle, when suddenly the sun comes out and you see yourself looking up out of the water. Don't worry—you haven't entered the Twilight Zone. You're just experiencing the reflection of light!

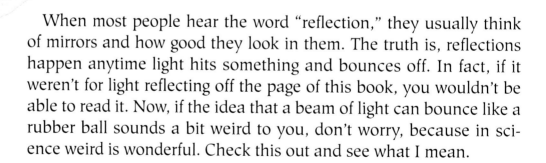

When most people hear the word "reflection," they usually think of mirrors and how good they look in them. The truth is, reflections happen anytime light hits something and bounces off. In fact, if it weren't for light reflecting off the page of this book, you wouldn't be able to read it. Now, if the idea that a beam of light can bounce like a rubber ball sounds a bit weird to you, don't worry, because in science weird is wonderful. Check this out and see what I mean.

flashlight

dark room

Go into a really dark room with a flashlight and close the door. With all the lights off, you can't see a thing! Now turn on the flashlight and sweep it back and forth across the room. As you do, different parts of the room suddenly become visible, but only for the split second when the light hits them. What's happening is that when the light hits the stuff in the room, it bounces back toward your eye. Unless light reflects off something, you can't see it!

Actually, there are two different types of reflection. The kind that happens in a mirror is called regular or perfect reflection. This can happen only when conditions are just right. The more common type of reflection (the kind that lets us see all the stuff in the world around us) is called diffuse reflection.

Here's an experiment that might shed a little light on the difference between the two types of reflection. You'll need a sheet of smooth aluminum foil, a table, and your face. Lay the sheet of foil flat on a tabletop with the shiny side up. Bring your face right down next to the foil and take a close look. What do you see?

smooth aluminum foil

table

Unless you're a close relative of Count Dracula, you should see your reflection in the foil.

Now take the foil and crumple it up a bit, but be careful not to rip it. Smooth it back out and look into it again.

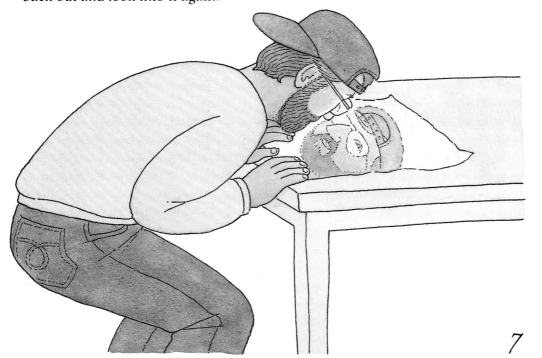

Regular reflection: the way light bounces when it hits a smooth surface, such as a mirror.

Diffuse reflection: the way light bounces irregularly when it hits a rough surface, such as this book, a ball, or your hand.

7

When you look at crumpled aluminum foil, your reflection is all broken up. In fact, you may not see your face at all—just bits and pieces or different colored patches. In the experiment, you changed a surface from smooth to rough and so changed the way the light bounces off it. When a beam of light hits a really smooth, shiny object such as the smooth aluminum foil, all the parts of the beam bounce off in the same exact way. It's predictable. But when light bounces off a rough surface, it bounces all over the place.

smooth concrete wall

5 balls

rough concrete wall

Try this. First, get 4 of your friends and 5 balls. Line up in front of a smooth concrete wall. Then, all of you throw your balls straight at the wall. What happens?

All the balls should bounce off in about the same way.

Now, instead of throwing them against a smooth wall, throw the balls against a rough brick wall with lots of cracks in it. What happens?

Each ball will probably go bouncing off in a different direction.

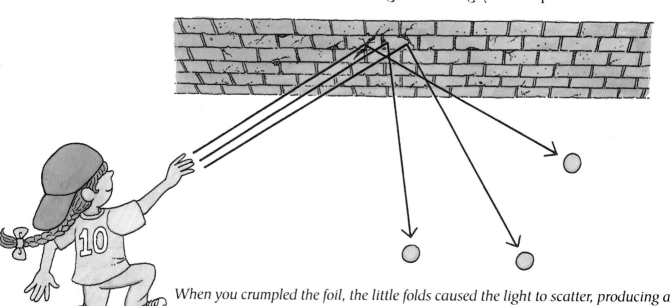

When you crumpled the foil, the little folds caused the light to scatter, producing a diffuse reflection, in the same way that the balls get bounced unpredictably off a rough wall.

To get a little better understanding of how regular and diffuse reflection work, you have to dive a little deeper into exactly what light is and how it travels from one place to another. To put it simply, light is a form of energy. It gets work done and makes stuff move. Compared with other common energy sources, such as electricity and nuclear power, most light energy is fairly weak and not very concentrated. As a result, its use is limited to things equipped with special light sensors, such as our eyes or the leaves of green plants.

When light travels from a point source, such as a light bulb or the sun, it moves out in pulses of energy called waves. These energy waves are strongest near the light, but they spread out and get weaker as they travel out in space. Eventually, they reach a point where you can't see the light anymore. It's sort of like throwing a rock into a pond. Where the rock hits the water, the waves are full, but as they spread out, they get smaller and smaller, until they finally fade away.

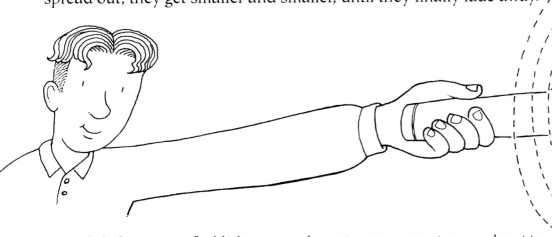

When light leaves your flashlight, it spreads out in waves as water spreads out in waves when you throw a rock into a pond.

You can build a simple light-wave model in your bathroom. All you need is a bathtub or sink filled about halfway with water. Hold the bar of soap in your hand and use it to gently tap the surface of the water near the middle of the tub. Do you see the waves moving out from the center? They may be very small. Watch closely. Keep tapping the water and watch the waves as they hit the side of the tub. They all bounce off in the same way. This is regular reflection in action.

bathtub or sink half full of water

table

new bar of soap

irregular object

To see how diffuse reflection works, you'll need something that floats and has an irregular surface, such as a toy boat. Place the object in one corner of the tub and start the wave action again. What happens to the waves this time?

This time, when the waves hit the surface of the irregular object, they should bounce off and scatter in many different directions.

That's diffuse reflection!

In order for something to be a mirror, it must produce regular reflection. That means that it must be smooth and shiny. Most mirrors are made out of a piece of glass or plastic with a silver-colored coating on the back. You may have noticed from time to time that really old mirrors have places on them that no longer reflect. That's because some of the silver backing has peeled off.

Things don't have to be mirrors in order to produce regular reflections, though. Many common objects do a perfectly good job, including smooth aluminum foil, the chrome bumper of your neighbor's old Chevy, and a window with a dark background behind it.

Next time you're sitting inside at night, try taking a look out a window with the lights on in the room. Stay at least 6 feet (2 meters) from the window. What do you see?

a window in a lit room at night

If the streetlights outside aren't too bright, the only thing you'll see is yourself! The dark background behind the glass, combined with the light reflecting off the front, turns the window into a mirror.

Now that you've explored what makes a mirror work, let's dig a little deeper into some of the cool things that mirrors can do. If you've ever taken a close-up look at your reflection in a mirror, you've probably noticed that things are a little mixed up. To check out what I mean, do the next experiment.

Print your name in big block letters on the paper and hold it up to the mirror. Look at the letters in the mirror. What do you see?

small, flat mirror

piece of paper

pencil

They're backward! Mirrors reverse images! That's why you can use one to decode the messages in this book.

If you hold the mirror up to your face and place a finger on the right side of your nose, on which side is your mirror twin holding his or her nose?

The left!

To discover why this happens, do the next experiment.

Take the paper and fold it exactly in half. Open it up and use the ruler to draw a straight line down the center of the fold. Now lay the paper flat on a table so that the line is coming right toward you. Stand the mirror up on its edge so that it is facing you, and place it right across the line. When you look into the mirror, the line should appear to continue from the paper right into the mirror.

ruler

paper

pencil

small, flat mirror

11

Slowly tilt the mirror back and forth across the line, changing the angle it makes with the line. You should see the line appear to bend in the middle, where it meets the mirror. The greater the angle between the line and the mirror, the more the line appears to bend! See if you can use the mirror to turn the line into the corner of a square. Or maybe tilt the mirror so that the line appears to jump off the paper, or to go into the table.

Angle of incidence: the angle at which light hits a surface.

Angle of reflection: the angle at which light reflects off a surface.

After doing the experiment, you may come to a startling conclusion. Whatever angle you hold the mirror across the line, the line you see in the mirror appears to go at the exact same angle, only backward. Congratulations! You just discovered one of the fundamental natural laws of science! Whatever angle light strikes a mirror at, it bounces off at the exact same angle. In science lingo you say the angle of incidence (strike) is equal to the angle of reflection (bounce).

To get a better understanding of exactly why this happens, you must return to your dark room with a flashlight.

flashlight

dark room

mirror on a wall or door

This time, you'll also need a mirror attached to either a door or a wall. Stand about 4 feet (a bit over a meter) in front of the mirror and hold your flashlight at eye level, pointing at the mirror. Then turn on the flashlight. Duck! The light should bounce off the mirror and hit you right in the eye! Now, take two steps to your right, so that you are standing off to one side of the mirror. Shine the light in the mirror again. Where does the reflected light beam go?

Pow!

The light should bounce over to the left of the mirror.

Move farther to the right of the mirror. Where does the reflected light go?

The reflected beam should bounce farther off to the left.

Now move back to the original place in front of the mirror and take two steps to the left. Where does the beam bounce?

If you said right, you're right!

Reflecting light beams off a mirror is just like hitting a handball against a smooth wall. If you want the ball to come straight back to you, you must hit it straight into the wall directly in front of you. If you want to send the ball off to the other side of the court, you must hit it off the wall at an angle. If you understand handball, then mirrors are a snap!

13

SPOTLIGHT ON:
Leonardo da Vinci, Mirror Writing, and the Mona Lisa

It's hard to say exactly who invented the mirror, but it probably was some cave people who glanced into a puddle of water and realized that the people looking back were really themselves. As long as 7,500 years ago, people were making "natural" mirrors by polishing special stones; later, as technology developed, they used shiny pieces of metal, including copper and bronze.

Glass mirrors with a silver backing were developed by the ancient Greeks about 2,000 years ago, but it wasn't until 1835 that modern glass mirrors were finally designed by a German scientist named Justus von Liebig.

Even though he didn't have the benefits of modern technology, probably the greatest innovator when it came to using mirrors was Leonardo da Vinci, scientist, artist, and all-around Renaissance type of guy! Leonardo's fascination with mirrors was probably due to his early training as an artist. Leonardo was 15 years old in 1467, when he was sent to live and work with the great artist Andrea del Verrocchio in the city of Florence, Italy. There Leonardo not only learned how to paint and draw but was taught sculpture, too. As he began to develop his own artistic style, Leonardo also began to take a fuller view of the world around him. He felt that the eyes were the most important part of the body. In fact, he believed that if you looked at something long enough you could figure out how it worked.

Symmetrical: made up of mirror images.

Using his artist's eye, Leonardo began to explore the way the world worked around him. He realized that most natural objects, including most living things, were symmetrical—that is, they could be split into parts that looked like one another. Looking into a mirror, Leonardo saw symmetry. Here's what he discovered.

14

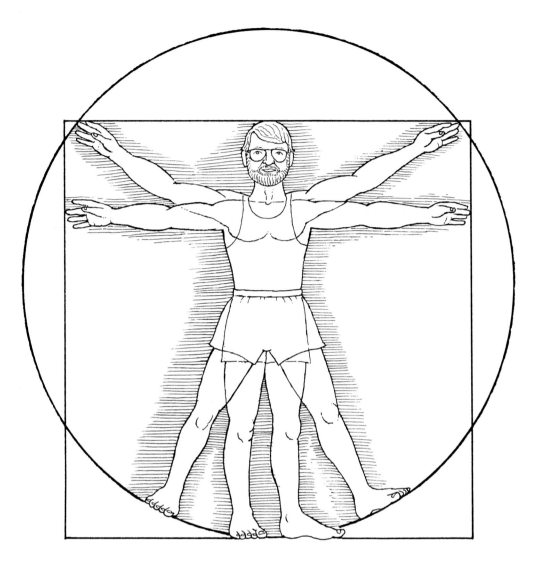

If you were to start at your head and split your body right down the middle, you would find that you are made up of two equal halves. With only minor differences, the right side of your body and the left side of your body are perfect matches for each other, except that they are reversed. Try putting your two hands together so that the thumb and pinky of one hand exactly line up with the thumb and pinky of the other. The only way you can do it is if you put them palm to palm or back to back. Now put one of your hands flat up against a mirror. You see the exact same symmetry as with your two hands! In fact, when people talk about body symmetry, we often say that our right and left sides are "mirror images."

Perhaps it was his fascination with symmetry, or maybe he just liked looking at himself, but Leonardo did literally thousands of experiments with mirrors. He developed a new type of art in which he used curved mirrors to make distorted drawings come back into focus. He became so obsessed with mirrors that almost all his scientific notes and observations were written so that they could only be read correctly in a mirror (like the answers in this book). Some people think that Leonardo's ultimate expression of mirror mania happened in one of his most famous paintings, the *Mona Lisa*. For years people tried to figure out who the woman model was that Leonardo painted in the picture. Using a computer and some drawings of Leonardo himself, a group of scientists think they found the answer. They think the woman model wasn't a woman at all! They think Leonardo painted a mirror image of his own face and simply changed the hair and clothes!

16

2

How Can Multiple Mirrors Change an Image?

Have you ever been shopping for clothes and stepped into one of those little changing rooms only to find yourself surrounded by a bizillion reflections of yourself? It can be quite a shock until you realize that you're really looking into three or four different mirrors set around you. Since mirrors reflect light in such a perfect, regular way, you can put several mirrors together and actually reflect a reflection.

How many reflections of yourself can you see when you stand in a dressing room?
Does it change from one store's dressing room to another?

By bouncing light off more than one mirror, you can do all sorts of cool things, including seeing around corners! Here's a quick little experiment to help you focus in on what I'm talking about.

hand-held mirror

wall mirror

You'll need a hand-held mirror, a wall mirror, and a brightly lit room. Stand about 1 foot (30 centimeters) away from the wall mirror. Smile . . . you look marvelous! Take the second mirror and turn it backward so that it is facing the first one about 6 inches (15 centimeters) from your nose. Look over the back of the second mirror and stare into the one facing you. If everything is lined up correctly, you should see about a dozen pairs of eyes looking at you! You are looking down a tunnel of light!

Have you ever before seen the effect you got in this experiment? How about when you get a haircut and the hair stylist holds up a mirror behind you so that you can see the back of your head? What's happening is that the more distant mirror reflects your image into the closer mirror, which in turn reflects it back to the back mirror, which reflects it back to the front one, and so on, until the reflection finally fades. The image gets smaller each time because the distance between your face and the mirrors increases every time the image is reflected.

See what happens if you move the two mirrors closer together or farther apart. Do the sizes of the reflections change? How about the number of images you see? With a little practice, you'll find that this simple setup can give you all sorts of weird effects!

One really cool toy that uses this same basic idea is the kaleidoscope. You can make your own human kaleidoscope by using two hand-held mirrors.

18

Here's what to do. Take two mirrors and face them directly at you so they are side by side, about 6 inches (15 centimeters) from your face. You should see one reflection of your face split in the middle where the two mirrors join. Now slowly move the outer edges of the mirrors toward each other so that they form a V. You should see more images of your face starting to appear. Finally, you'll see two full images of your face.

Keep going. What happens to the number of images as the angle between the two mirrors gets smaller? Depending on the size of the mirrors you use, you can get dozens of reflections, but they will all have the same symmetry or pattern.

When toy companies build kaleidoscopes, they use this exact same idea. Inside the kaleidoscope's round tube are two or more mirrors set at angles to each other. By reflecting little bits of colored glass or sand, the mirrors create a series of spectacular images in the light.

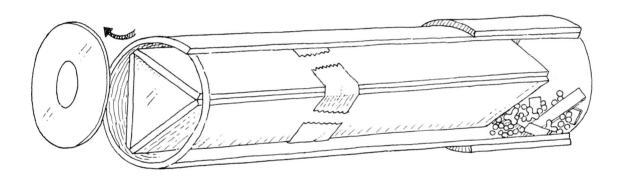

While multiple mirrors can be a lot of fun, they also can be very useful. In the early 1800s a new type of sea vessel called a submarine was just starting to make a splash. Because it could go under water, a sub could sneak up on an enemy ship without being seen. The only problem was that when they were under water, the submarine's crew couldn't see where they were going. As you can imagine, this could be really embarrassing, especially if they surfaced near an enemy ship! In 1854, a group of French engineers came up with a clever idea. By fitting two mirrors at angles in opposite ends of a long tube, they could scan the surface above without being seen. The periscope was born.

2 small mirrors

cardboard milk or orange-juice carton

tape

scissors

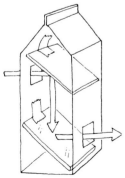

To build your own simple periscope, you'll need two small mirrors (like those found in a makeup compact), a cardboard milk or orange-juice carton, some tape, and a pair of scissors. Start by cutting a square hole in one side of the carton, near the top. Cut at least 3 inches (8 centimeters) down and remove the piece of cardboard. Flip the container over and cut a similar hole in the bottom of the container on the opposite side.

Take one of the mirrors and place it inside the bottom of the container opposite the hole, so that it is facing you and tilted up at a 45-degree angle. Use the tape to secure it tightly in place.

Flip the carton over and place the second mirror in the top opening exactly as you did the first. If you hold the periscope up to your eye and look at the bottom mirror, you should see what's in front of the top mirror.

To test it out and align the mirrors properly, you'll need a flashlight. Make the room dark and lay your periscope flat on a tabletop. Shine the flashlight straight into the hole at the bottom of the carton and watch where the beam goes. If all works well, the beam should come out the top hole. If not, try adjusting the angle of the mirrors. In no time you should be seeing around corners and over walls!

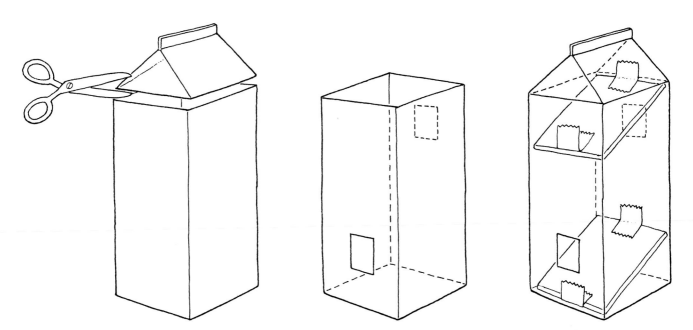

The top should be opened all the way to allow maneuvering inside. You can tape it up again when you're done.

So far, we've reflected only on the behavior of flat mirrors, but there is no reason that a curved surface can't be a regular reflector too. The truth is, we use curved mirrors all the time, although most people don't even realize it. Have you ever looked in the mirror on the passenger side door of a car and seen the words "Warning, objects in mirror are closer than they appear"? If you have, then you've looked into a curved mirror. But how can a mirror change how far away an object appears to be? Here's an experiment that should help to sort things out.

shiny teaspoon

flat hand-held mirror

Hold a flat hand-held mirror still about 6 inches (15 centimeters) from your face and look directly into it. You should see a close-up view of your nose and eyes, but not much else. The reflection of your head is blocking you from seeing what's behind you. Now, hold a very shiny teaspoon up in the exact place you held the mirror and look into the back of it. What do you see?

If it's shiny enough, you should still see your nose and eyes, but they'll look a little funny—sort of stretched out. If you are a very careful observer, you'll also see a lot more of what's behind you and a little of what's off to the sides, too.

Now hold the mirror in one hand and the teaspoon in the other. Place them side by side about 6 inches (15 centimeters) from your eyes. Which reflector gives you a closer look at your eyes?

If you said the flat mirror, you are right. The reflection in the teaspoon seems to be pushed way into the background.

So what's going on here? As you discovered before, all of the light that hits a plane or flat mirror bounces back at the exact same angle that it strikes the mirror. As a result the image is reversed, but the distance behind the mirror the object appears to be is exactly equal to the distance in front of the mirror the object actually is. In curved mirrors, things don't work this way.

The back of a teaspoon is curved out; in science lingo we call this a convex surface. A concave surface, on the other hand, is the exact opposite. It curves in, like the front of the teaspoon. On a convex mirror, the light that hits the surface at an angle gets bounced off at a wider angle. To use our handball idea again, if you hit the ball off of a curved wall instead of a flat one, the ball will go shooting off at a much larger angle.

Convex: curved out.
Concave: curved in.

Convex mirrors allow drivers of cars to see a wide area off to the side and help to eliminate any "blind spots" that regular flat mirrors can't show. Convex mirrors are also used by banks and store owners so that one person behind the counter can keep an eye on the whole room instead of just one small piece of it.

You are the sales clerk. Can you find the shoplifter in this convex mirror and stop the crime?

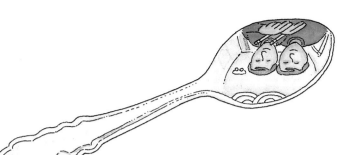

Okay, so if convex mirrors spread things out and make things look farther away, what do you suppose concave mirrors do? Let's go back to the teaspoon to find out.

This time turn the teaspoon around so you are looking into the front side, which is curved in. Instead of one image, you may see two or three, and to make matters worse, they're upside down. Try to focus on the largest of the reflections and you will see a nice close-up of your eye.

shiny teaspoon

Because they're curved in, concave mirrors cause all of the light that hits them to come together at a point. We call this point the focal point. Since all the light is concentrated at the focal point, the image looks bigger than it would in a flat mirror.

Focal point: where light comes together at a point.

SPOTLIGHT ON:
Isaac Newton and the Reflecting Telescope

When most people hear the name Isaac Newton, they think of gravity and falling apples. The truth is, Newton explored much more, including why objects move and how light behaves.

He even invented calculus, a type of math.

Isaac Newton was born on Christmas Day in the year 1642 in a small farmhouse in England. His father had died several months before he was born, so young Isaac was raised by his mother and grandmother.

Isaac was quite sickly as a child and spent a great deal of time in bed reading to himself. He had a hard time concentrating in school, so when he was 14, Isaac's mother took him out, and he became a full-time farmer. Unfortunately, Isaac had a hard time concentrating on farming too. Instead of doing his chores, he would spend his time in some far-off corner of the farm reading and trying to figure out why the world worked the way it did. Fortunately for him, his uncle saw his potential as a thinker and arranged for him to study at Cambridge University.

Over the next 30 years, Isaac Newton completely changed the way scientists viewed the world around them. He demonstrated that the universe wasn't some mystical thing, but was actually very orderly and followed a set of natural laws. As part of his studies, he discovered how curved mirrors could be used to either concentrate or spread out light. You can conduct one of his most important experiments.

shiny teaspoon
flashlight
table
dark room

Lay the flashlight flat on the table and turn it on. You should see the beam of light spread out across the table. Now place the back of the teaspoon about 6 inches (15 centimeters) in front of the flashlight. If you angle the spoon so that the reflected light hits the tabletop, you'll see that the reflected beam of light is spread wider than the one coming from the flashlight. As we discovered before, convex mirrors spread the light out.

Now turn the teaspoon around so that the concave surface is facing the flashlight. If you angle the spoon so that the reflected beam hits the tabletop, you should see a very bright spot a few inches in front of the flashlight. That point is the focal point, where all the light comes together.

After doing this experiment with curved mirrors and a candle, Newton realized that he could design a telescope that would take in the light from distant stars and concentrate it so that the stars looked bigger. By putting a curved mirror at one end of a tube and an angled mirror at the other, he was able to obtain better images of the moon and planets than any seen before.

While many of today's telescopes are much larger and much more advanced then Newton's, many still use this same basic design that he developed more than 300 years ago!

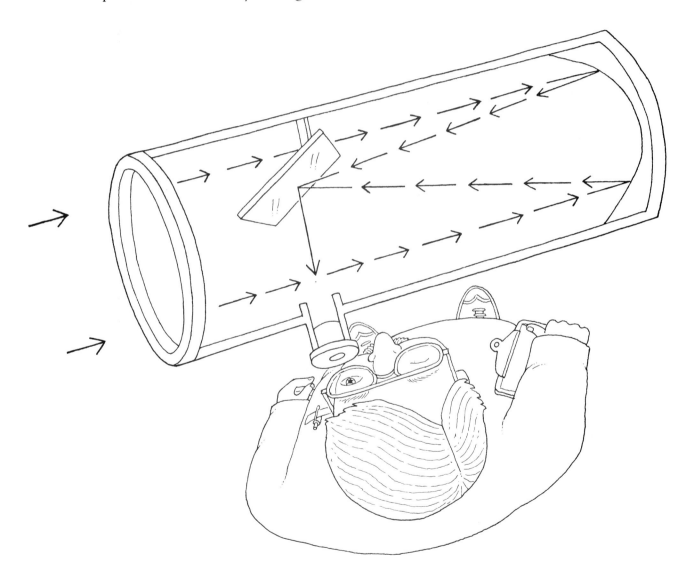

3

How Does Light Bend?

Refraction: the bending of light.

Have you ever been strolling along the beach and spied something really interesting lying in the water? Maybe it's a brightly colored rock or a cool-looking shell. Anyway, you reach down to pick it up, and suddenly it's gone! As you stand back to look, you see it again, but no matter how many times you try to pick it up, it always seems to be out of your grasp. What you've experienced is another property of light, called refraction, or the bending of light.

In the last chapter, you read about how light moves in straight lines and travels in energy pulses called waves. Light also travels really fast—about 186,000 miles (300,000 kilometers) per second through outer space, where there is no air.

As it turns out, when light travels through different materials, such as air or glass or water, it changes speed, and it's this change of speed that can make a light beam bend! To see how it happens, try this experiment.

Place a clear container on a table and fill it about 3/4 full with water. Stir in 3 or 4 drops of milk, so the water looks just slightly cloudy. Don't use too much milk or else the experiment won't work. Make the room very dark, and hold a very bright flashlight above the container so that it shines straight down on the surface of the water from the top. You should see the beam going through the water as the light comes out of the flashlight. Now slowly tilt the flashlight so that the beam hits the top of the water at an angle. What do you see?

flashlight

dark room

table

large clear glass container

water

milk

Where the light strikes the water, you should see the beam of light bend down a little bit. The greater the angle between the water and the flashlight, the more the light beam seems to bend.

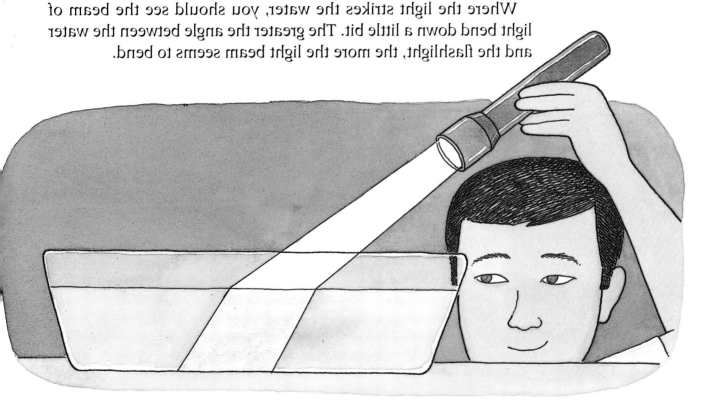

To understand why this happens, you have to think about riding on a pair of roller skates. Let's say you're cruising down a nice hill on some really smooth pavement. Suddenly you notice a patch of grass in front of you. You try to miss it, but unfortunately your left roller skate runs over the grass while your right one stays on the pavement.

27

What happens to you? Well, if you manage to keep your balance, you'll find that your body will turn to the left and you'll continue to run over the grass.

The reason this happens is that the wheels of the skates roll faster on pavement than on grass. Since your left skate suddenly slows down but your right skate keeps going at the same speed, your body is forced to make a left turn. If the situation were reversed and your right skate suddenly slowed down, you would find that you'd make a right turn instead.

Don't try this at home!

Transparent: *able to allow light through without blurring; clear.*

Well, this is exactly what happens to a beam of light when it has to travel from one transparent material to another. Because the beam from the flashlight is wide, the bottom of the beam hits the surface of the water before the top does. Light moves through water pretty fast—about 140,000 miles (230,000 kilometers) per second—but not nearly as fast as it does through the air. Since the bottom of the light beam slows down but the top of the beam keeps going, the entire beam is forced to turn down into the water, just like you on your roller skates.

So why doesn't the beam bend when you hold it straight down? Well, if we go back to our roller-skate idea, think of what would happen if you were cruising down the pavement and all of a sudden it ended in a big patch of grass. If both skates hit the grass at the exact same time, they would both slow down together. Instead of turning, you would probably fall flat on your face!

The same thing happens with the light beam. When you hold it straight down into the water, all of the light waves hit the water at the exact same time. Since they are all slowed together, the beam simply slows down instead of bending. Your eyes can't see the light slowing down, so the beam seems pretty much the same.

You can see this same effect with reflected light bouncing off an object under water.

Stick a straw into a clear glass half full of water. If you hold the straw straight up and down, it doesn't appear to bend when it enters the water, although it does look a little bigger. (We'll get into why this happens a little later on.)

Tilt the straw so that it enters the water at an angle, and look at it from the side. What happens?

clear glass

drinking straw

The straw will appear to break in half.

Because the light bouncing off the straw under water takes a little longer to reach your eye than the light bouncing off the straw in the air, your brain "sees" them as two different straws. This effect helps to explain why you can't pick up that shell or shiny stone under water so easily. Let's try another experiment.

coffee mug

table

penny

glass full of water

Place a penny in the bottom of the coffee mug and place the mug on the table near the edge. Kneel down in front of the table so that, as you look into the empty mug, the front rim of the mug just blocks the penny from your view. Your nose should be about 2 inches (5 centimeters) from the rim of the mug. Without moving the position of your head, begin to fill the mug with water from the glass. (It might be easier if you get a friend to help you.) As the water level in the mug goes up, what do you see?

The penny should pop into view.

It seems like magic, but there's no magic to it at all—it's simply refraction of light at play! What's happening is that when you are looking into the empty mug, the light reflecting off the penny is traveling through the air and toward your eye. Since light travels in straight lines, the rim of the cup blocks this light from reaching your eye, and you can't see the penny.

As you add water to the mug, the light bouncing off the penny must first travel through the water and then through the air before it gets to your eye. Since you are looking through the water at an angle, the light bouncing off the penny reaches the top of the water and bends toward your eye. Because the light is bent, the penny becomes visible again. The penny hasn't moved and neither has your eye—only the light has!

Now let's go back to our shell under water. As you look down, your brain tells you that the shell is straight in front of you because you normally see things in straight lines. Unfortunately, the light reflecting off the shell has been bent where it leaves the water, so the shell is actually closer to you than you think. The only way you can pick it up is to stand directly above the shell and look straight down into the water. That way, all the light waves reflecting off the shell hit the air at the same time, and they speed up together without bending.

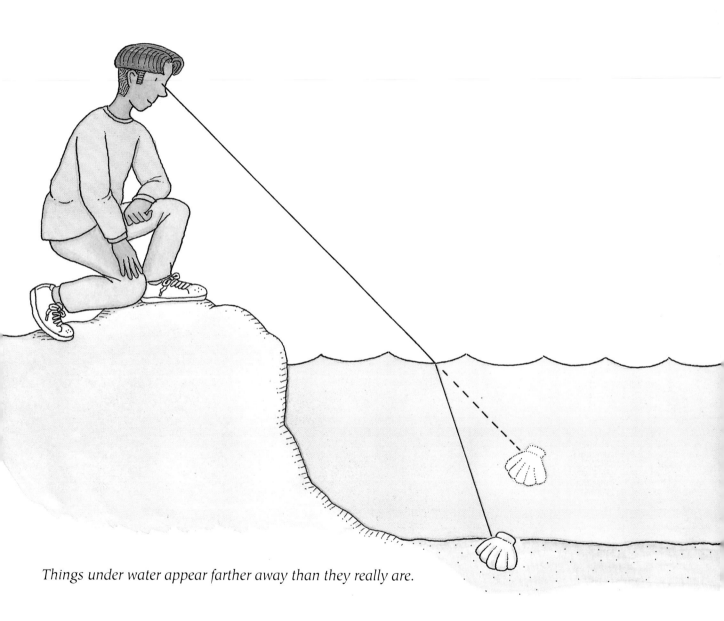

Things under water appear farther away than they really are.

4

How Do Lenses Work?

Simply stated, a lens is any piece of clear material that bends light in a regular, predictable way. Lenses bend light exactly the way the water in the coffee mug we used in the last experiment does, except instead of having just one angle, they have a whole bunch of angles connected together. Lenses also come in many different shapes and sizes—from the tiniest magnifier to the giant glass covering of a lighthouse. You can find lenses in thousands of different devices, including cameras, eyeglasses, telescopes, and microscopes. In fact, if it weren't for lenses, you couldn't read this book, because you've got one in each of your eyes!

To make a lens, all you need is a curved piece of glass that has a changing thickness. You can try a simple lens experiment using a clear glass of water, a flashlight, a dark room, and a comb. That's right. I said a comb!

clear glass full of water

flashlight

table

dark room

comb

Lay a flashlight down flat on a table and turn it on. Make the room dark, and you should see the beam of light spreading across the tabletop. Now hold a comb about 1 inch (2 centimeters) in front of the light so that the light beam shines through the teeth. You should see a bunch of narrow light beams coming out of the back of the comb.

Place the glass of water about 1 inch (2 centimeters) in front of the comb. What happens to the light beams now?

As the beams come out the back side of the glass, they should bend in toward one another and meet at a point.

If you think you've seen this type of thing before, you're right! When you held the flashlight up to the concave reflector, you brought the beam to a focal point. The point where all the light beams meet behind the glass is also a focal point.

Different-shaped lenses have different focal points. The glass you are using is called a biconvex lens because both of the edges that the light passes through are curved out. A concave lens is a piece of glass with at least one of the edges curved in. Instead of bringing the light together at a point, a concave lens actually spreads it out more, so there is no focal point! If you think back to the section on curved reflectors, you might have realized something strange. With mirrors, a concave shape brought the light together, while a convex shape spread it out. In lenses, it's exactly the opposite! The convex lens concentrates the light, while the concave one makes it more spread out.

To see how different-shaped lenses change the focal point of light, you can do a simple experiment.

Biconvex lens: a lens that has both sides curved out.

Concave lens: a lens with at least one edge curved in

Lay a flashlight on a table and turn it on. Make the room dark and you should see the beam spreading out across the table. Place the narrow glass of water 1 inch (2 centimeters) in front of the flashlight, so the beam shines through it. What do you see?

flashlight

narrow clear glass of water

wide clear glass of water

dark room

table

ruler

comb (optional)

You should see the light beam focus a small distance behind the glass.

Using the ruler, measure how far the focal point is from the front of the flashlight. Now, remove the narrow glass and place the wide glass 1 inch (2 centimeters) in front of the light. What happens to the focal point?

If you said that it moves out, you're right. Depending on how wide the second glass is, the new focal point should be anywhere from a few inches to a few feet (10 to 100 centimeters) farther from the flashlight.

The reason for the change in the focal point has to do with how much of a curve the light from the flashlight has to go through. The greater the curve on the edge of a convex lens, the closer the focal point will be.

Being able to use different-shaped lenses to either concentrate or spread out light becomes very useful, especially for people whose vision isn't exactly perfect. When you look at an object, light enters your eye through the lens. The lens of your eye is curved out (it's convex), so the light is focused behind the lens on the back of your eye.

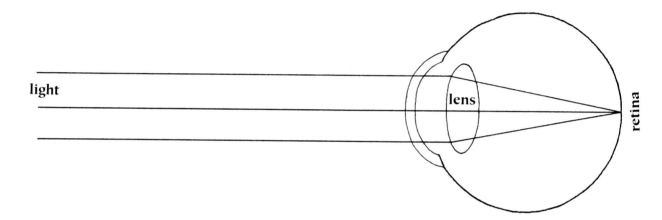

If everything in your eye is working correctly, the image of what you are looking at should be focused directly on your retina. From here, the image is sent to the brain through the optic nerve, and you see.

What happens if the lens of your eye gets bent out of shape? This happens quite frequently, and as a result, people need to be fitted with special high-tech correcting lenses. The common name for these devices is glasses.

Let's suppose that the lens of your eye is a little more rounded than it should be. Based on the experiments with the water glasses, a greater curve means that the focal point gets pulled forward in front of your retina. As a result, you would see objects that are close up fine, but things far away would be blurry, or out of focus. In science lingo, you would be considered nearsighted, because you could see only close-up objects well. To correct the problem, you would need glasses that had concave lenses in them to spread the light more and push the focal point farther back.

Let's say the opposite happens, and the lens in your eye becomes too flat. Well, now the focal point is pushed behind the retina. You can see distant things fine, but close-up objects become fuzzy. Now your vision is said to be farsighted. To correct this problem, you would need an eyeglass lens that is concave. That way, the light will come together a little more before it reaches the lens in your eye, and the focal point will be pulled forward.

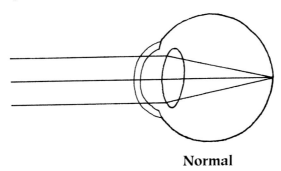

Normal

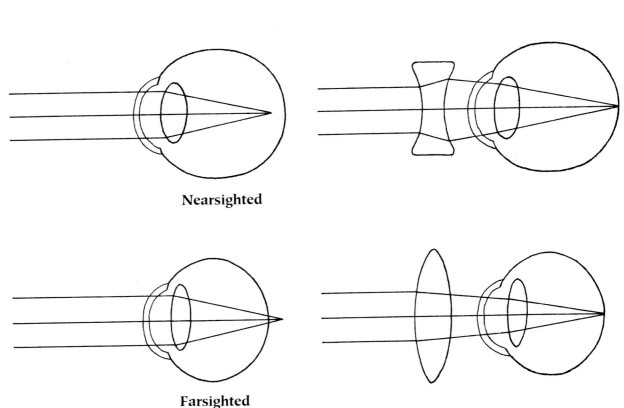

Nearsighted

Farsighted

SPOTLIGHT ON:
Ben Franklin and Bifocal Glasses

Today, eyeglasses are so common that it's hard to believe that people ever got along without them. Actually, the use of lenses to help correct vision goes back to the Roman emperor Nero, who reportedly used a piece of natural emerald as a lens to help him watch gladiator games around A.D. 50.

In the beginning, most lenses were made from natural clear crystals such as quartz or beryl. As you might imagine, finding crystals the right shape to get the job done was a difficult task, so only the most important members of society ever got a pair of glasses. By the 1300s manufactured glass had become more common, and the use of eyeglasses spread quickly.

By the late 1700s eyeglasses were so common that many people owned two pairs: one for reading up close, and one for seeing at a distance. Having to constantly change back and forth between two different types of glasses was a real pain, so the American inventor, scientist, and statesman Benjamin Franklin came up with a more practical solution.

Taking the lenses from two different glasses, he proceeded to cut each in half lengthwise. He then mounted the two types of lenses together in a special frame, and in 1784 bifocal glasses were born. To use them, all a person had to do was look through the lower lens to see close up, and look through the upper lens to see far away.

For Ben Franklin, the development of the bifocal was just one thing in a long list of accomplishments. In addition to his work with lenses, Franklin experimented with electricity and was the first to build a lightning rod. To help keep people warm in the winter, he developed a new type of wood-burning stove that is still in use today. As a statesman and politician, Franklin helped to draft the Declaration of Independence and was involved in setting up the Constitutional Convention of 1787. Not bad for a guy who spent his spare time flying kites!

5

How Do Lenses Magnify?

If you think back to when you did the straw-in-the-glass-of-water experiment in Chapter 3, you may remember that when you held the straw straight up and down in the water, it didn't appear to bend. It seemed to get bigger. Convex lenses not only bring light to a focal point, but they also make objects viewed through them look bigger—a process called magnification.

To see how the curve of the lens changes the magnification of an object, you'll need a clear glass half full of water and a straw.

Magnification: the process of making a thing look bigger by passing the light coming from it through a lens.

Place the straw in the middle of the glass so that it is straight up and down. If you look closely, you'll see that the straw appears to get bigger at the point where it enters the water. Slowly slide the straw to the front of the glass. You should see it start to get smaller. Now slide it to the back of the glass. The straw will appear to get bigger again.

clear glass half full of water

straw

To understand how the lens magnifies the straw, you first have to understand what magnification is. If you think about it, the simplest way to make something look bigger is to hold it closer to your eye. If you take a penny and hold it between two fingers about 3 inches (7 centimeters) from your face, it looks a lot bigger than if you hold it out 2 feet (60 centimeters) away. The reason it looks bigger close up is that you are viewing it through a much larger angle than when it is far away.

small angle

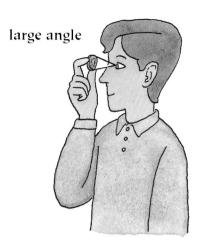

large angle

By bending the light rays coming from the object, a magnifier actually increases the angle at which your eye sees it. When you look through the water at the straw, the straw looks bigger because the water in the glass bends the light toward your eye. The farther back you move the straw, the bigger the angle the light makes with your eye.

If you look at a penny with a magnifying glass, the same thing happens. The magnifying glass keeps the light coming from the penny from spreading out too much, so you see it at a wider angle.

Using a magnifying glass changes the angle at which you see things.

Glasses of water and magnifying glasses aren't the only things that can make an object look bigger. All you need is a transparent object with a convex surface and—presto—you've got a magnifier.

Here's an experiment you can try using nothing more than a drop of water and a newspaper. You might also want to get a piece of clear plastic wrap to keep the paper from getting wet.

newspaper

plastic wrap

water

Spread a sheet of newspaper out on a tabletop and lay a piece of clear plastic over a section of it. Sprinkle a few drops of water on the plastic wrap and look at the letters underneath. Compare the size of the print under the water drops with the other print. Which letters look bigger?

The ones under the drops.

If you place your eye at tabletop level and take a close look at the water drops from the side, you'll see that they are curved up on top, just like the surface of a magnifying glass. Since they have a convex surface, water drops are mini-magnifiers!

Of course, real magnifying glasses can do things that water drops can't do. If you happen to have a magnifying glass, try this next experiment.

Hold the magnifying glass up near one eye and take a look at something close up. Your hand is a good object. You'll see all the grooves and lines, and you might even see some dead skin cells.

magnifying glass

While you're holding the magnifying glass near your eye, shift your view to some far-off object in the room. A clock or picture on a distant wall works well. Slowly move the glass away from your eye and watch what happens. At first the object will appear really fuzzy, but as you move the magnifier farther away from your eye, the image will begin to get clearer. Somewhere along the line you should notice that the object appears to flip upside down. No, you're not suddenly standing on your head. What happens is that light rays coming from the object pass through the lens and cross in space, making what you're looking at appear upside down.

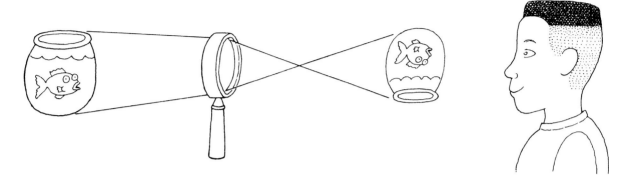

Now, if you think that this kind of thing happens only on rare occasions, think again. Since the lens in your eye is a convex lens too, everything you see is actually upside down on your retina. Don't worry, though—that's the way your brain likes it. When the upside-down image reaches your brain, it turns it right side up again, interprets color and depth, and—presto—you have a wonderful view of the world around you!

SPOTLIGHT ON:

Hans Lippershay, Galileo Galilei, and the Refracting Telescope

Earlier, you read about Isaac Newton and his experiments that led to his building the first reflecting telescope. Thirty-six years before Newton was even born, however, two scientists working in different parts of Europe developed the refracting telescope, which forever changed the way we here on Earth view the universe.

The story begins in what is now Holland in the year 1608, when a 38-year-old eyeglass maker named Hans Lippershay had just gotten a new shipment of lenses. As the story goes, two children playing in his shop started fooling with the lenses, and in the process discovered something amazing. Just by chance, they held a concave lens up to their eyes while looking through a second convex lens stretched out at arm's length. They discovered that the weather vane on a building across town suddenly appeared extremely close up.

Realizing that the discovery could be put to practical use, Lippershay mounted the two lenses inside a hollow tube, and the kijker, which is Dutch for "looker," was born. He sold the first one to the Dutch government, which wanted to use it for spying on ships far out at sea. Later, in Paris, the king of France bought one, and the news of the new device quickly spread.

While traveling in the city of Venice, Italy, in the spring of 1609, Galileo Galilei, a scientist and inventor, learned about the looker. When he returned to his home at the University of Padua later that year, he built his own telescope, which was much better than Lippershay's.

Galileo developed a special method for shaping and testing the lenses he used, and by the fall of 1609, he had a telescope that could magnify a distant object about 33 times.

In the beginning, the telescope had been used strictly for military purposes, but Galileo had other ideas. From the time he was a young boy, he was interested in the stars and tried to figure out how they moved. At this time, people in Europe believed that Earth was at the center of the universe and that the sun, moon, planets, and stars all went around us. A new theory offered by a Polish astronomer named Nicolaus Copernicus suggested that Earth was simply another planet going around the sun. Unfortunately, there was no proof to support this new idea.

Using his new telescope, Galileo looked up at the night sky and discovered the proof needed to defend the Copernican theory. He published his finding in a book called *The Starry Messenger* in 1610, and in 1613 he began to publicly defend the new theory developed by Copernicus.

By 1616, Galileo had caused so much commotion that he was ordered to Rome to appear in front of the Pope, who ordered him never to teach about or defend the theory of Copernicus again. Galileo knew he was right, but he didn't take any action, because in those days, if you went against the Church, you might be put to death!

Finally, in 1632 he wrote another book, called *Dialogue Concerning the Two Chief World Systems,* where he strongly defended the idea that the sun, not Earth, was the center of the solar system. As a result, he was put on trial and sentenced to life in prison, although he was later allowed to spend his time under house arrest. Galileo died in 1642 at the age of 78, blind and defeated, and still locked in his villa.

Even though Galileo never saw the truth accepted, he knew in his heart he was right. Later that year, Isaac Newton was born in England, and it was his theory of gravity that would eventually prove Galileo right! Because of the telescope and Galileo's work, the Copernican system was eventually accepted and people's ideas about the structure of the entire universe were changed!

6

Where Does Color Come From?

Any discussion of bending and bouncing light wouldn't be complete unless we asked the age-old question, Why is the sky blue? Well, you might say it's because it reflects the ocean. A good guess, but unfortunately not true. In reality, the sky isn't blue at all—it's clear! It only looks blue because of the way that the light coming through it is scattered by water vapor and other gases in the air. In short, we have color because of the bouncing and bending of light!

If you look at a beam of light coming from the sun or from a flashlight, it appears to be white. It turns out that ordinary light is not white at all, but is really a combination of colors blended together. This fact was first discovered by Isaac Newton back in the late 1600s. He found that if you take a beam of light and pass it through a special lens called a prism, the white light divides into seven major color bands.

prism

Dispersion: the separation of the different colors that make up light.

Spectrum: the band of colors that appears when white light passes through a prism.

You were reading earlier about how light moves in vibrations called waves. Well, each of the seven colors—red, orange, yellow, green, blue, indigo, and violet—travels in different-sized waves. Because a prism is a lens, it bends the white light going through it just enough so that the different-sized waves are sorted from one another. As the light goes through the glass, the red light is bent the least and the violet is bent the most. This process of sorting out white light is called dispersion. The band of colors that results is called a spectrum.

Even if you don't have a prism, you can divide white light into colors just as Isaac Newton did.

baking dish

water

table

flashlight

hand-held mirror

You'll need a shallow baking dish with about 3/4 inch (2 centimeters) of water in it, a table, a strong flashlight, and a small hand-held mirror. Place the pan of water on a table and lean the mirror up on one end so that it is half in and half out of the water. Now make the room as dark as you can and shine the flashlight so it hits the part of the mirror that's under water. You might have to play around with the angle of the light a little, but after a few seconds—presto—you should see a rainbow—that is, a spectrum—appear somewhere on a nearby wall or ceiling.

How does a mirror in water split light into colors? Since the light has to go into the water at an angle, it bends as it hits the water. When the bent beam of light hits the mirror, it bounces off the surface. Then the beam of light bends again as it leaves the water. This time it is bent so much that colors appear.

Okay, so we explained where color comes from—it comes from light. If you don't have light, you don't have color. But why do certain objects always appear to be the same color? Why is the sky blue?

As white sunlight passes through our atmosphere, it strikes tiny little particles of dust and water vapor. When it hits these particles, the light is scattered in all different directions. We say it becomes diffuse. *Diffuse: scattered.* Earlier on, we said that light bouncing off any rough surface gets scattered by diffuse reflection. Well, the same thing happens in the sky. Instead of bouncing back into space, sunlight gets scattered before it reaches the surface.

When white sunlight starts bouncing off these particles, the different colors in it begin to scatter in different amounts. The blue light, since it bends more (think of the prism), is scattered more than the red light. When the blue light finally reaches our eyes, it has been scattered all over the sky. The sky looks like it is blue!

To see for yourself why scattered light looks blue, you can try this experiment.

flashlight
clear jar
water
milk

You'll need a strong flashlight, a clear jar (an old clean mayonnaise jar works fine for this), some water, and some milk. Fill the jar almost to the top with water and add 3 or 4 drops of milk. Stir the milk in so that it is evenly spread through the water. The water will now look a little cloudy. (The milk represents the dust, water vapor, and gases found in the atmosphere.) Turn on the flashlight and shine it through the side of the jar. If you look where the beam of the flashlight goes through the water, you see that the water appears slightly blue. It's not! You know it's really cloudy white, but the milk scatters enough of the light to make it look blue!

Final Note

After all is said and done, the real pleasure that comes from the bouncing and bending of light is in the way we see the world. By observation we learn that the true beauty of science is the art of discovery.

Keep looking up, and enjoy what you see!

Books

Aronson, Billy. *Scientific Goofs: Adventures Along the Crooked Trail to Truth.* New York: Scientific American Books for Young Readers (W. H. Freeman), 1994.

Cassidy, John, and The Exploratorium. *Explorabook.* Palo Alto, Cal.: Klutz Press, 1991.

Fleisher, Paul. *Secrets of the Universe: Discovering the Universal Laws of Science.* New York: Atheneum (Macmillan), 1987.

Macaulay, David. *The Way Things Work.* Boston: Houghton Mifflin, 1988.

Nye, Bill. *Bill Nye the Science Guy's Big Blast of Science.* Reading, Mass.: Addison-Wesley, 1993.

VanCleave, Janice P. *Physics for Every Kid.* New York: John Wiley & Sons, 1991.

Video

Facts of Light. 3-2-1 Classroom Contact.
Available from G.P.N. 1-800-228-4630.

Television

Dr. Dad's PH³: Phantastic Physical Phenomena. Louisiana Public Broadcasting. Check your public TV and cable listings or contact Louisiana Public Broadcasting to find out where to catch it in your area. This is my show! Steve.